This book is dedicated to
all the people who choose
to look on the bright side of life
There is love wherever you look

# The Optimistic Heart

a collection of poems
by CJ FitzGerald

# Our Hearts all Love and Break the Same Way

There's an experience I had that I want to share with you
It was a couple of decades ago, maybe a few

It was very, very late – almost midnight
I arrived at Midway on a delayed flight

I had traveled alone, as I often did then
What time would I get home? I didn't know when

I was waiting with others for the Economy Lot Shuttle
Exhausted folks queuing up in a scattered huddle

No one spoke to each other, not a single word
All different people from all over the world

Certainly different upbringings and religious views
Just all of us standing there, looking down at our shoes

The shuttle arrived and we all collapsed into our seats
Still staring at nothing so we didn't have to speak

Some music was playing on the shuttle radio
Even at this hour, the driver was a happy fellow

The song "My Girl" comes on and I couldn't help myself
I started to softly sing along, alone at first, then I got help

The man next to me joined in, with a soulful voice and louder
And wouldn't you know it, soon we were all singing together!

*continued ...*

The refrain starts –
"I guess you say, what can make me feel this way . . ."
A spontaneous joyful connection of strangers at play

We're all laughing and singing - our very own show
On an Economy Lot Shuttle in south Chicago

We might have started our short journey apprehensive
for a while
Now we were all united by that universal language
Music and a smile

We arrived at our stop just as the song ended,
and we parted ways
Our moment had passed, but I'll remember it always

I said a little prayer for each of those passengers that
night
May they always feel safe, and may their hearts always
be light

I still think of them to this day, because that moment
touched my life
We're all on this shuttle together, so let's live with less
strife

There are more good than bad in folks this big world
Our hearts all break the same way, so let's help
heal the hurt

Earth belongs to Love and it's not ours to fight about
It's amazing to me that we all can't figure this out

*continued . . .*

Open your heart and you'll see it seeks love just like mine
If we could all choose love, and not hate, we could all be fine

I was raised in a broken home, but to me we were whole
We were taught to never hurt another soul

It's easy to be a victim of circumstance and decide to be cruel
Because in your life, bad things have happened to you

It takes hope to rise above this rage, and happily live
Stop acting entitled, and be brave enough to give

It seems when we all pray, our Gods are the same
I know mine would not ask me to kill in Their name

You may call your God a different name than I do
Whatever it is, I know they bring comfort to you

And if you don't agree with anything I say
I want to tell you that it's really okay

I won't insult you or hurt you if you disagree
I will be kind to you, as your feelings should be free

Many times it seems it's tolerance we lack
Let's keep hope alive and have each other's backs

Pray for love and Grace and hearts at ease
Most of all, pray for Peace

# The Writing Man

So I was in Greek Town - this was the late '70s
I'm at this bar waiting for my first taste of Gyros
(I'm not sure I liked it)

Anyway I look across the bar
There's this intense man, writing hard and fast
On a yellow legal pad

He wore round, wire-rimmed glasses, his face etched with a
Fierce expression
Jaw clenched
He's probably around 40, lanky yet muscular
His head was made of shaggy wayward, dull blond curls that
danced with every forceful
Stroke of his pen

He pressed so hard, you'd think he was going to
carve into the bar top
Shredding (like Prince's guitar)
He's writing furiously, maniacally
He wrote without a pause, a constant
Stream of Thought

With every dot of his "i", I felt like I was
Being shoved hard with one finger
Like being provoked
I sort of involuntarily reeled back a bit

*continued . . .*

With every swift cross of his "t", I felt somehow aroused
I understood him so we'll - the lyrics to "Killing me Softly"
going through my head (Roberta Flack version)
Atavistic
He MUST write
NOW

He's got to get it all said before he forgets
He MUST get it all on paper, and OUT of his head
I was riveted watching him
I coveted his intensity

I wanted to somehow acknowledge our kinship
but knew I never could
It's not proper etiquette between writers to interrupt
The Flow

I've been there myself -
I grappled for a surface to write on
A napkin, my hand
Anything!
Where's a pen!
It just seems genius at the time

More than anything, I wanted to read what he wrote
(I new I never would)
But it surely must have been about love or rage
Sometimes they look the same

*continued . . .*

After about 10 minutes, he stopped abruptly
He leaned back in his bar stool
Hooked one arm over the back
Rested his pen against his lower lip
Gazed up at the ceiling and pondered

I knew what he was thinking - A better way to phrase it
Editing is inevitable (it seriously **never** ends)

And so it commenced
With just as much ferociousness
Almost as if he were punishing himself
And so he was

# Young

I'm sitting on the front porch enjoying a summer evening
A car speeds by, windows down, music blasting
It reminded me of an old friend
We were 19
Immortal

We were recklessly speeding south on Rt. 83
In his little MG convertible
It was late - around midnight
Our hair was flying around chaotic
Singing along to Springsteen's "Rosalita"
What a rush
We were laughing hard
It was thrilling

Oh the way he shifted gears
Hands so gifted - piano genius
He was tall, muscular and slim
Long blond hair
Light blue eyes

Robust laugh, but so soft spoken
We were very good friends
Sometimes, when I caught him looking at me
I felt adored and desired all at once
He became a composer - appropriate and perfect

Wherever he is now
I hope he's well and ridiculously happy

# Hope

Her heart is racing but not from fear
From joy!

Is she dreaming? She's not sure
Because it's all so vivid, so vibrant
She knows you can't see star trails with the naked eye
But there they are!
Swirling, interwoven, dancing
On the background of a velvet navy sky

They look like the Creator's love, like a Van Gogh painting
They feel like the happy souls of every loving mother have
joined together

And they're pouring out peace, joy
A nurturing, blanket over the Earth

Now she sees a cloud symphony
She opens her arms to embrace them
All their music
The world is a festival

Even if it is a dream, she knows all of this happens every day
And she feels hope

# You are Loved

When you're struggling, remember
By your very nature
You are necessary

You were born into this world
Exactly
As devinely designed
You were born in your ultimate form
As natural as a sunrise

Express yourself as you wish
Love whomever your heart desires
You're here, so you are
Essential

When you feel no one is thinking of you
If you feel inconsequential
Remember the Universe loves you and needs you

We are all linked by human kindness
We are all the same *race*
*Human*

*continued . . .*

We are all *of* each other
From different parts of the Earth

Treat yourself with the
Reverence
You were created to
Deserve

Know this:
You are already a Divine masterpiece
You are loved

# Life

Your life will consist of
Beginnings
And Endings
And Possibilities
And Tragedies
And Elation
And Opportunities
And Regrets
And Creativity
And Misunderstandings
And Mistakes
And Apologies
And Love
And Grief
There is no great loss without great love
The world is equally
Terrifying and magnificent
If you can manage the terrifying
It's far more magnificent
So go on with your bad self
Go live that life

# Rythm of the Day

If you listen carefully, you'll hear music constantly
The swish of thick summer leaves in a warm breeze
Squirrels chirping to each other
Birds peeping to their young
Water bubbling playfully in a brook
Water roaring mightily over a mountain fall
In the ocean breeze, palm trees sashay away
Waves gently trickle or crash at the shore
A whimsical crunch of  fall leaves
The whistle of hurricane winds
The deep low moan of tornado winds
Laughter and crying come in so many octaves
The rhythmic rumble of a train rushing by
The snap of Acorns as they fall to the ground
The tubular sound of water lapping on a boat
The call of hawks and other birds
The melancholy coo of doves
The pounding of hard rain on your roof
The shuffle of boots walking through snow
The howl of coyotes
The symphony of a thunderstorm
And the crack of lightning
The tink-tink of rain on metal
The splash of a dolphin and their cute chatter
The boom of a whale breaching and their soulful call
The crackle of a bonfire
The chirp of crickets as the sun falls
You can add to this list endlessly
Music is everywhere
What will be your song of the day?

## Vortex of Awesomeosity

Oh the love I have witnessed today from my front porch

Friends and families walking together into town

Parents walking home from the train and kids running into their arms

Neighbors stopping by to chat for awhile

Our mail person, Dee, gives a smile and kind words

Music and laughter from backyards around us

Some young men playing guitars and trumpets on their
Own front porch steps

A big brother helping his little brother learn to ride his bike

Dogs romping around each other while their owners chat

Birds nesting in our tree

An elderly couple walking by hand in hand

Walkers resting on the bench kindly built by my neighbor
Across the street

The scent of bonfires and BBQ fill up the night

Our home is in a loving neighborhood
It's fun to be us!

# The Eclipse

Oh the magnificence of today
Of the Earth
Of the Sun and Moon dancing
Of the Galaxy
Of the Universe
Of Love
Of Community
The world stands still to watch the wonder
Skies turn to sunset
Then to night
Bird songs stop and cricket songs start
Crescent shadows everywhere
Planets and constellations waving hello
Connection
Surrender
Peace

# Happy Place

I'm wearing my Grandpa's Hawaiian shirt from the '50's
It has coconut shell buttons

I'm sitting on the front porch swing
Alone on a hot summer Saturday evening
Sipping a cocktail
While it rains

Listening to soul music
And watching the trees in their party pants
Dance in the storm

Am I the old lady on the corner
That sits on her porch, even during a rainstorm?

Indeed I am
And I feel peaceful

# People are Wackadoo

Each is unique
The best thing you can do is to let them
Be
Whomever they are
Just as **you** are

Love them as they choose to be
With their quirks
With their mistakes
With their talents
With their loves

Hell - if you look at yourself
You're a bit wackadoo too

I know I'm not everyone's favorite
Even if I wish I were

And I am grateful
For those who give me grace
And include me - even love me
Regardless
of my very own
Wackadooness

# Spring Drivers

Everyone driving by smiling with windows open wide
Some cars have kids that are laughing and waving hello
Some have music blasting
Some shout happy greetings
Some teens shout profanities
Some have a dog on their lap
Some people's hands are wind surfing out the window
Hair flying free
And here I sit on the front porch swing
Watching so much joy for warmer weather
Drive right on by
Increasing my smile

# Circles

Everything is at its most beautiful
at it's crescendo -
Just before it dies:
An ocean wave
A sunset
A sunrise
A starry night
Autumn leaves
Flowers
Our souls
Childhood
Innocence
A love story
A smile
A hearty laugh
A raindrop
A snowflake
A Thunderstorm
A bonfire
You get the drift
Everything fades out
But they all begin again
And oh the joy in experiencing them over and over

# To my Grandchildren

I am your Nana, and I love the sky
The sun and the moon and the clouds floating by
I love to gaze at the stars at night
Connecting our hearts with all my might
I will share all these wonders with you
Your whole family loves the sky too
You're made us stardust and so am I
We were instantly woven in the blink of an eye
Before I even heard about you
You were a person I already knew
You've been in my dreams as long as I remember
I am your Nana, and I'll love you forever

# The Morton Arboretum

Where do you go when your world seems awry?
Things are amiss, and you don't know why

Or maybe you're brimming with a joyful energy
And you're seeking somewhere lovely to be

There's no reason to hide
We were born to be outside!

You can go for a walk in this strong and safe place
Where the seasons unfold with a peaceful grace

A walk thru the trees is the best therapy around
Where Nature's soothing songs will abound

Like the rush of the wind through early summer trees
Or the whimsical crunch of October's leaves

Or the symphony of birds that glide through the air
Soon you'll be breathing calmly, without care

Maybe you'll think of how we're all woven together
And take care for each other, no matter the weather

And if you want to discuss what's deep inside thee
Talk to the trees! They will always agree!

# Estrangement

Life brings heartbreaking relationship challenges
I never thought you'd be one of them
I've soul-searched long and hard about our abrupt
Ending
Let's start over today
I know better now
I know the part I played in the past
I made you feel inconsequential when you were young
In my attempt at protecting you
From a life full of struggles
Instead, that's exactly what you lived
I'm so deeply, utterly sorry
Do you know the part you play in the present?
Are you also sorry?
Let's figure it out
I miss you and your family
Immensely
Achingly
I'm reaching out to you
Will you please reach back?

# Cosmic

What do we look like from celestial skies?
To the sun, moon and planets?
Do people on earth look like twinkling stars?
Each of us are own galaxy
Made of stardust
So maybe, when it's your birthday
You shine brighter than anyone else
Maybe the planets anticipate your extra glow once a year
Like the meteor showers we await
Maybe we look like a sparkling galaxy of souls at night
And the Cosmos look at us in wonder too

# Keep the Faith

When you are giving yourself grace
When you're seeking forgiveness
When you're having a crisis of Faith
When you're drowning in your worries and need direction
When you're saying your prayers
When you're expressing your gratitude
What Diety did you learn to turn to?
Was it Alah, God, Jesus, Lord, The Almighty, Budda
Alpha and Omega, King of Kings, Father, Mother Mary,
Universe
Or simply
***Love***
Whatever your faith, it's the right one for you
Because no matter what you call your
Own soul's Creator and Savior
They are all one and the same
They have many names
They unconditionally love you for just existing
They are neither gender nor man made
They are all omnipotent
We all pray to the very same higher power
You learn throughout your life what brings you the most
Comfort and redemption
What brings you the most joy
What brings you the most peace
The definition of God is universal
We all pray to the same One
You must simply Keep the Faith
Keep your Faith

# About the Author

CJ's fascination with the outdoors started early. She is always looking up, and is a proud member of the Cloud Appreciation Society. She has told stories about the Sun and Moon, and has written poetry for as long as she can remember. She enjoys writing many genres. "Miss Sun's Twinkle School," is her first published Children's book. Her second Children's book is "Cora's Cloud Club" featuring her own photos. She has lived in California, Michigan, Missouri and currently Illinois. After retiring from a corporate career, she is now enjoying work at The Morton Arboretum in Lisle, IL. You can find her anywhere outside enjoying a good hike and taking nature photos. She also loves to sit on her front porch swing reading or talking with neighbors. She calls her neighborhood, "The Vortex of Awsomeosity." With a life full of moves and travel, she's currently enjoying writing stores for her 12 grandchildren. Much of her writing is about the people she meets, and her observations as an Alpha (generation) Nana. Her family motto is, "It's Fun to be Us!" Her first poetry book for adults is "The Optimistic Heart." She hopes her messages are comforting, encouraging, thought-provoking and informative.
Contact: itsfun2beus@gmail.com

www.ingramcontent.com/pod-product-compliance
Lightning Source LLC
Chambersburg PA
CBRC090837120626
46551CB00007B/687